Henry's 8th book

The 8th book collection

To my family and my beloved GOD, who has uplifted me
And to Sarah... my sister whom I love to dedicate this book to her...
Sarah is now the OFFICIAL CO-author!!!
Congratulations Sarah!!! my gem!!!
Thank you Sarah!!!

BOOK 8

Catalog

BOOK 8 2
KING ALMIGHTY 5
GLORY TO GLORY..6
DEAR savior 8
Sister 9
THE SHORE 10
Mission 12
The days beginning..14
GRACE..15
Night song 24
Cleopatra 25
NATURES MORNING..28
THE RIGHTEOUS ONE 30
Truly you are… 31

Henry's 8th book

— 3 —

Light house… 32
Twilight rhyme..34
DAWN 35
Wedding supper 37
Ode to the morning… 38
HOPES HILL 40
AND TIME WAS BORN! 41
Tick tock… 42
The panther… 43
PRAISE TO THE KING! 45
The starry night 46
Fire light 47
LOVE 48
COBY...50
OH! MORNING LIGHT! 59
To you my Annie… 60
RAIN… 62
Suffering 63
Shores of twilight..65
ODD OR EVEN 66
DAVID 68
DESIRE…..77
THE BEAUTY OF CREATION 79
THE BEGININNG … 80
The Dreams We Dream…..................................81

— 4 —

Title	Page
THE LORDS LOVE…	82
And it was the day…	83
The New Beginning…	85
THE ONE TRUE CONSTANT:	86
the stars…	87
TO THE BROKEN HEART	92
To the solemn night…	93
WE ARE!!!	94
THE DAWN…	96
WHOM SHALL I SEND	97
YOU…	99
And the day began…	101
Twilight rhyme	102
DAWN	104
NIGHT SKY	105
Sunset journey	107
DUSK	108
Morns glory	110
A star Is born	112
The little boy	114
Arthur	116
Oh my friend!	126
In the deep…	127

Henry's 8th book

— 5 —
KING ALMIGHTY

The day... and the joy... the night and its heaviness... every part of the pain there is hope in my suffering your comfort in my pain my hope in my suffering is your word preserves my life
So many have suffered... everyone has onward eyes longing for hope but greater than hope is love tis love and our saviour that is love is sweet and loving and there is no end to his rescuing love and his grace is with men... his hands are gentle his caress is beautiful... there truly is no one like him... the power of a lion, the humility of a lamb... who is this light of day who is this king of glory the king almighty the day proclaims his brightness and the night speaks of his vastness and

his rule! How wonderful how great the lord almighty, king of glory king of ages YOUR LOVE IS NEVER ENDING...

GLORY TO GLORY

Is there hope in you? For the sun rises and sets in one day and that one day becomes night... the stars shine and display all your glory so as far as the glory to glory you reign over the night to the day for ever on the stars shine and you glorify the sky from day to night the moonlit   midnight clouds flow overhead... and your glory in the morning, all of it tells your eternal story from hope to hope glory to glory day to day evening to evening fades from

Henry's 8th book

— 7 —

night to day- the only way... for you are great every-time you stay for you in us and us in you shines to so be true your glory forever, my needs are made better and you cover me in warmth like a warm sweater comfortable and cozy so that I am dozy thus you and I are free to fly in our sky and walk the shores so great to our eternal fate and onwards to heavens gates. Till I am near to the throne where i no more moan to the gates of home GOD REST MY SOUL...
Blessings...

Henry's 8th book

— 8 —
<u>*DEAR savior*</u>

Dear savior times are difficult... I miss you my heart yearns for you...people all around the world are suffering only a reminder that we do not belong here... a soft answer turns away great wrath... For you I hold dear...I comfort your presence is a warm sparkle of life... in my heart I am very dry and desperate for you...all the things that I have suffered in my life have been guiding me back to you...
I need you please help me come back to you... please come back??? I am alone and poor and needy   you are my all in all... blessings...

Henry's 8th book

— 9 —

Sister

Dear soul your all around beautiful and glorious I truly love all your ways...your sweet and beautiful... everything that's surrounds you is lavender and purple!you are the excellent person you truly are a wonder to me... for how wonderful are all your works! And with all your ways you glorify all that is with that that is around you your grace filled walk is a glorious light that shines the way in darkness!!! Your star stunned beauty follows you... you are altogether beautiful and glorious... GRACE BE TO YOU!!! my beloved Sarah! Peace be with you... I love you Sarah, I love you forever...

Henry's 8th book

— 10 —

For Sarah my dearest sister

THE SHORE

The mid day was a comfortable cool breeze the two walked with their 3 kids on the shores... the mother was happy and comfortable on the beach... the father rejoicing in his bride on this occasion as they walked... the wind with the edition of the tide cooled their feet in the sandles of the day the children were galloping thru the waves on the shore... the sun occasionally peeking thru the clouds the pup   in a tromp following the children... then! As the sun reached the western horizon... the clouds passed for just a glimpse, a glimpse of splendor and majesty of the sun settling with golden red and orange colors that covered the sky   a glorious bold setting of a horizon and as the family walked the beach their hearts settled in peace   with the sun setting with their hearts...

FIN

Mission

The round sphere was eclipsing the blue giant and gracefully shone a blue circle to this newly born globe of living color for now and for now to bloom new life! The blue sun shone its brilliance around the eclipsed new born planet! As the craft of space, this missile of space-time circled this new found planet the shifting eclipse made an orbit around this lovely blue and green sparkling orb as the sunrise of a sphere crept around the orb: "come in space command…"
"we have arrived"

— 13 —

"space command read you loud and clear, space command to the iris prepare for landing"
"ready and waiting"

Soon the craft prepared for landing as it braced for   its landing sequence
"brace for atmospheric impact!! as the forces pulled and pushed on the ship the craft went out from signal range for space command...
When it had landed com was re-established...
"space command, do you copy?"
"read you loud and clear..."
"space command , landing successful"
"gathering materials for instrumentation and scientific study"
"we read over and out..."
As they were done excavating for research they took off and headed home bound and blasting off they went!!!

Henry's 8th book

— 14 —

The days beginning

As the book is looked
the reading is seen as the sight brings
bright
the yearning brings learning
And for want brings lots to forge a form
That talks as everything for want brings
the hope for a walk
Yet a walk so learned that the years are
earned and sought after for as the deer
pants
For the babbling, the babbling brooks...
for the books are looked
at the reading brings dreams

*only to catch the day in the morning
a yearning for crying as the day brings
bright at first light
for the day is bright in GODS eternal
might!
And the day in its beginning is the
mornings ending
and with that the sun and its shining!*

GRACE

*As she walked along the path the sun was
rising as the flowers were blossoming on
the trees...
The wind was a cool breeze on the
country path... there, in the beauty of the*

Henry's 8th book

— 16 —

sun rise, the earthy tree roots bared bulges on the thick and rugged ground and the sun shone on the wind swept path with the sun glistening on the leaves swept by the soft breeze...

Her name was grace, and grace was taking a trek on her favorite path as she walked in the morning
With the sun rising over head it shone thru the mist beam of golden light piercing   the foggy air which had a crisp feel to it... as she walked to her home the sun greeted the day, she was reaching her home and as she opened the door, took her jacket off... turned on the lights turned on some soft classic music and cleaned her hands...

She looked in the mirror, sighed...
She was watching face...

All the trials she had been thru as she dazed into her past as she eyed off into the distance
As a young girl talking to her mom...
"mommy why is daddy mad?"
" honey?", with a tear filled face she choked on her words saying,"things are gonna be different im so sorry im so sorry please be strong for me can you please do this one thing for me,be strong for mommy...."
That was the day their father left them there to suffer and abandon his daughter to tearing pain and weeping...

Later that year at school...
The girls ganged up on grace and were spitefully teasing her
"leave me alone!"
"please!"

"HEY LEAVE HER ALONE!"

*The playground monitor joined in... "GIT!"
They broke off the assault
"why do you allow them to tease you, grace?"
"i cant stop them im helpless!"
"miss grace you are never helpless as long as you ask for help and are willing to receive it..."*

"run along"

School was very hard on her

When she was in high school she suffered loneliness except for a friend named Cassie who was always by her side...

*"Cassie? Are you busy?" "no what is it?"
They had fun in the park on Saturdays playing yard games*

*But again something tragic happened
Cassie was with her other friends in a car accident...
She was brutally killed and taken from grace in a drunk driving accident...
Grace grieved for a whole year...
"mommy? Hold me..." she broke with much weeping and the terror struck her heart and the pain went deep
"why does everyone leave me? She was full of tears and it tore her heart to shreds... two years later she was in college, sadly she with all her pain had become addicted to drugs to cope from years and years of great fatigue and depression people mocked her for it which only drug her deeper in to addiction*

Later having been caught in possession with a high alcohol content she was put thru mandatory counseling and sentenced into non formal probation for 2 years

That was when they realized where all this grief was coming from
"WHY DADDY!!? WHY DADDY!!! WHY DID YOU LEAVE ME??!!"
Tears poured from her searing eyes screaming trashing her vocal cords....
The counselors were humbled by her terror and felt grieved and helpless to heal her...
And they were as humiliated as she was... love was the only answer... there in the brink of her falling off the metaphorical cliff, LOVE HAD COME FOR HER!

That night in a dream :
"GRACE..." in the dark she opened her eyes... the voice spoke: "grace I knew you from the moment I saw you in your mothers womb I have seen your great distress and misery, your love lost your hope undone and your deep pain..."

Henry's 8th book

— 21 —

"GRACE?" "I AM THAT I AM"

"i love you with a love like no other my love cannot be described by human words I have predestined you to my home this love I give you I give to you MY LIFE!!! free of any charge for your hope faith love and future"
"GRACE! WAKE UP!"

When she did there were tears streaming down her face...
She touched her face in astonishment!
SHE, BUT FOR ONLY A MOMENT WAS IN TOTAL UNBELIEF!
The phone rang...
Still shaken she felt insecure but in this knowledge, she felt hope and peace...
"HE- hello?"
"HI GRACE! You wanted to meet me?"
"who's this"

Henry's 8th book

— 22 —

"James"
"oh OK..."
When they met he "counseled her about GOD"

"Yeah GODS our friend, im so exited about him... do you know the LORD?"
"yeah? Who's that! She scoffed...
"why he is the great I AM!"
"waa waa wait, what did you say?"
"what didn't you know?"
"no its just a dream..." she told him the dream
 he gasped

Later in the year they got serious with each other
But James became abusive and she lost hope... then they broke up
 But hope returned and she found the LORD again she felt peace again love in her heart for the   savior she was single

minded and whole hear-ted and leaned into the lord the I AM that she saw in her dream and found hope and faith there was peace in her heart and freedom that lasted for eternity

Thus she came into focus in the mirror as she gazed at the mirror she saw only grace grace physically spiritually and a loving heart and grace from the savior

Blessings...

Night song

The night was cool the stars glittered in the sky the crescent moon shone thru the night... as the wind blew a quiet breeze, the trees whistled from the wind as the ponderosas waved in the wind the owls hooted the coyotes whelped the crickets also could be heard... the sky was a clear sight to be seen....

And the pond in all its glory joined in the music of the night as a gentle song the deer still awake drinking from the brooks next to the pond, lifted her head to the music... the night was a beautiful example of what dreams could bring for the night creatures and all their calls to the night... As the sun became closer to the horizon the light took presidence over the darkness as the song of the night quieted for the morns glow and the morning began

Cleopatra

At sunset on the rugged old bench an old woman sat her name was Cleopatra and she was feeding the birds as she sat the birds surrounded her... they were cooing she tossed the seed in handfuls to the doves as the birds nibbled at her feet... as the sun set the breeze was slight... left alone by her family abandoned because of her husbands death the widow sighed but being valued by her creator she was loved by the great father of all

— 26 —

Her life was near end people passing by only frightened the cooing birds yet they trusted   Cleopatra and came back and with her cane, she walked home (a few blocks from the retirement RV park) The evening was raining out... the birds, flocking to her house... birdseed was in bird houses for the hungry birds as night fell it was extremely dark and windy... as she was dreaming she dreamed of all that would be and all that could be...

In her dream doves poured around her and she felt peace... she saw a faint but golden glowing figure coming up from the distance on the cool shores and he was dressed in marvelous white with a golden sash around his waist he had ruddy good looks very tall and a very handsome grin...

As he came up he said: "Cleopatra! Welcome home..."

"im not dreaming?"
"No ..." he chuckled...
The two were speaking as if in a pleasant dream and she gracefully entered her resting place

She woke up and there she was standing in front of a mirror she was astonished for she looked 18 again... she touched her face...
"Cleopatra? Your home... he smiled
OH! JESUS! IM BEAUTIFUL! I don't look a day over 20!
"He he.. you certainly are beautiful!"

"Jesus where are we?"
"heaven!, of course?"

That was the day the day that would never end it was like a beautiful dream That spanned all time

Henry's 8th book

— 28 —

There on top of the green flowing hills   a golden glowing city

The shining sky the golden paths the great temple of their father and the son... that was the day everything was always new!

Fin...

<u>NATURES MORNING</u>

The morning dew was sweet on the garden of tulips the rain had soaked the dew filled vegetation
All night...the birds sang a beautiful melody in the treetops as the sun was rising... the does and bucks slowly foraging thru the newly grown grass... the clouds a new and glorious   oranges and reds covered the sky, the morning mist above the mountains kept the firmament a cool breeze the day had just begun and it was beautiful the morning light shone piercing the fog with beams of golden light streaking across the sky and it was the Natures morning...

Henry's 8th book

— 30 —
<u>THE RIGHTEOUS ONE</u>

To the morning star... the star so great the evening and morning, it dominates... a little twinkle for now but a great shining in heaven!!! is there any lamb so precious as the morning bright?
In the evening and morning twilight? You are the beloved son and righteous one... you are the hope sought after the love in one true spirited faith... is there any majesty as you... we cry for you the world seeks a savior- a savior THEY WILL FIND! You are the anchor of hope your bride is ripe for harvest...
She is your loving doe thirsty for your beauty and love... for as a doe pants for the pure brook...

Henry's 8th book

— 31 —

Great love flows as sacrificial blood pours from your veins a pouring of your beautiful heart...
That doe, a fine maiden the church, awaits as the pleasure has been set before you...
For you!!!! are the great I AM!- the savior of the world!!!

Truly you are...

Dear Annie dear my own, my own beloved... how fair are your hands so delicate, skin so fair
Ode to my Ann! Your tender beautiful heart of love to me? Oh Annie? How you

shine in your beautiful heart... your tender look... your tender soft touch to my my heart your fingers a quiet touch how a fair maiden you are? We walk the shores in the morning... the cool breeze in daylight with patches of clouds covering the sun, we are one... you laugh truly you are a fair maiden a lovely woman
Time touched eternity is in your left hand beauty in your right.. truly you are grace and life, truly you are...

Light house...

There... on the shores, rocks on a great cliff, is a a shining light house

— 33 —

Guiding the way, keeping safe the seer the cold wind blows as the seas crash against the rocky shore...
A beacon of hope and life and peace... guiding the ocean bound crafts and people to safety...
Oh! This fair light! To all who see this guide! The light guides people home this messenger, and anchor and beacon- Jesus! Guides the way! And all who see this beacon are blessed with light and warmth and hope... as he shines the glory divine... no might can outshine his light! No power greater than his love... that beacon of hope reigns over his beloved sheep guiding his precious lambs to safety and joy for! They are the joy set before him and Jesus is the joy for all mankind... and they shall be together forever in peace love hope and joy...

Blessings...

Twilight rhyme

As the sun would rise the night has died and the twilight hides
Thus the morning greets the sun so sweet on the mountaintops those gentle mountaintops
So I gaze a glare so brave on the trees so great that the twinkling of the stars so dim   I see the mornings rim... a rainbow in the west as it bears its best... an army of colors a tapestry of glory that the morning cannot compare with such a

glorious glare the clouds part the bright sky the morning begins ans the twilight sings

And the day begins as the morning ends

Thus from every beginning, there is some beginnings end...
-Henry

DAWN

The moon was a bright orange disc in the sky... all the crickets were singing in the night scenery

There the stars were twinkling a chatter on a black backdrop. Lighting the sky like twinkling firefly's
As the earth spun the night stars flew over the canvas sky as the night time passed...
The moon slowly spun thru from horizon to horizon over the dark period...some parting clouds a deep and quiet ocean blue lit by the moon passed across the sky morphing as they went
A wind blew a cool chill on the surface of the earth...
The owls were excited for it... thew very beginning of the dawn had begun
Softly gently the moon's light had dimmed quietly and slowly dissipated along with the stars
Only to have the morning light replace and follow the night
A morning rainbow of rising color had engulfed the twilight the sun had risen

thus the moon was a faint crescent in the sky, the sun had risen and it was the dawn

Wedding supper

The bells shell rang as the melody sang... as the trumpet bulged, the movement echoed in the halls of gold and silver forever and eternity made clear that the father was near... when he spoke, the brightness was stoked and the angel cried out as a song loud... beauty was present as life was not silenced, a love like no other for one another... the wedding supper for the lamb for the time spanned, in heaven for the show bread had the leaven for the food for marriage was ready for the   mood and grace was embraced for the spirit holy and   love truly...

<u>***Ode to the morning...***</u>

Oh! The daylight... to the morning is anything so glorious? Such shine it covers the sky with light....
The beauty of it all... like the joyful morns cry! The glory shines! To liken a day with

joy the illumination of morns beauty... the one true father   shining his light   thru his son the glory of true wisdom... shines the love of the fathers heart... love shone bright illuminating every corned unseen till now! The LORDS GLORY in sacrificial love, blood pours as the dawn illuminates the last of the night... the victory won in that righteous one so glory be it to be the I am as the I AM glory to the father forever and ever

AMEN!

Henry's 8th book

— 40 —

<u>HOPES HILL</u>

There on a hill stands hope... this hope reaches to the heavens its justice like the oceans tide this hope is the hope of the world the hope for all mankind.. his love is beautifully eternal his compassion spans the stars in every galaxy his mercy is in loving favor... be blessed for you are special and well loved and deeply wanted... he is here for you... one hope for each and every one on earth... to be happy safe in his arms and comforted in the warm bed of sacrificial love from his heart...
THE LORD HAS NOT FORGOTTEN YOU...
he loves you with an unfailing love... for he is yours and you are his...

Blessings...

Henry's 8th book

— 41 —

AND TIME WAS BORN!

twas before the dawn of time... and there!!! in the blackness of the Abyss, was a bright, small, and warm sparkle of life... a glimmer in the UNBORN EYE! a pin prick of brilliant light a vision of hope a quiet birth of light... AND THERE!!! immediately after the pale blue sparkle as small as infinity... burst brilliant rays in all directions and vectors! THAT! birthed everything from nothingness and consumed by everything that was nothing before!!! dare this burning inferno!!! every single microscopic piece of the blasting expanse we call the universe!!!

every nana meter of rays pushing matter into existence!!! AND TIME WAS BORN!

Tick tock...

Tick tock
As the time unwinds
Tick tock
The gears wind
Tick tock
And as the clock minds
Tick tock
The time draws nigh
Tick tock

Henry's 8th book

— 43 —

The clock runs dry as the time dies
Tick tock
The alarm sings
Tick tock
The trumpet rings
Tick tock
Then, the end is well penned

The panther...

There in the deep abyss of the forest greenery of the ferns the flowers were opening of the bottom of the ferny forest... the sunlight casted its gaze seeping through the skylight from the top of the ferny roof tops of the lit forestry, there, deep in the jungle lay a pouncing panther... its vision slashing the bushes at his prey...ready to attack!!! bending at

attack position ready and eager... the rodent unaware of the silent but deadly danger lurking quietly behind him in the bushes... suddenly!!!! POUNCE!!!
The rodent cried for help!!! but no one to answer... the creature was snared by the deadly cat no one to save.... the panther eating his dying prey... and the panther gorging on his newly gathered meal...
the panther left the dead carcass gushing fresh and smelly blood left there for the scavengers... and the rodent's hope was cut off... the day ended with the scavengers eating the carcass and the sun along with the hope of that poor animal, had set...

Henry's 8th book

— 45 —
PRAISE TO THE KING!

in the midst of the mighty mass... and this tempered temple... is a mighty king and his cathedral... and HIS "seeing" goes forth from his "appraisal..." SEE! HOW THE PEOPLE FLEE! AS HE! wields... his SABER! of CHARTER! HE is the GREAT and BRAWNY LORD! with his THIGH! at his SWORD!!! and his COMMAND! at his WORD! to his majesty and might? there is NO NIGHT??? HIS ROYALTY! and all HIS GLORY rises with HIM in the MORNIN' and sets in an ETERNAL STORY!!! PRAISE TO THE KING! and to the LORD GOD, OUR FATHER! praise to their kingdom... "SANCTION' "be their" 'dominion'! may the LORD and KING be glorified! father GOD and King forever

The starry night

There, the stars were illuminating the night sky... as Anna sipped her chamomile tea, she sat on her favorite bright blue blanket and she lay before the night stars she sighed and watched the comets int the blackboard of the night... and there! The moon, shone brightly and the aura of the moon engulfed the surroundings... the stars sparkled in the night as as Anna slept on the grasses with her favorite puppy, "spot"... the pup curled up on her side... a cool wind blew on their backs as Anna curled up on her blanket and fell asleep her pup and her together and the moon slid across the sky

Fire light

The hour was dark... the night was wet and the rain was drizzling as the clouds poured rain... the lightnings thundered! And the sky crackled over the deep... Inside though, was a different story... While the lightning popped across the sky, the fire place crackled peacefully as the fire warmed the bedroom... The fires glow warmed the accent of the room and the

Henry's 8th book

— 48 —

bed was soft... as the storm Henry's fifth edition 33 thundered over head, the rain fell softly on the bedroom windows... they were sleeping... at a gentle rest... as they were happily asleep off to some dream scape the orange tabby cat happily nestled in between the cover that they slept in, it was night... As they dream-pt the storm surged overhead and they were happily unaware they slept to their hearts content... Blessings...

LOVE

all day long in loneliness I wait am very patient

— 49 —

i know you are deeply suffering and I understand with you I know you have been hurt in the past so? I suffer with you... my heart breaks for you and even when it breaks my heart to see you fight me and are mislead I suffer long for you while you leave me and after all the great pain you have caused me I see in you no wrong and I still care and pray for you and for you? I would die... to save you... do not fret? I have always been on your side and I know sometimes you lose control but I can calm the stormy sea in your heart I still love you and always will for my name is the great I AM...
Never give up...

COBY

The noon day sun was a brilliant ball of fire and it casted its light upon the people of the planet...
The people were happy and there joy-full peace... life was bright during that great time... there were, though groups of people unsettled and murmuring of the major issues of the planet... and like many there was one who stood up against freedom lovers and people of peace... his name was scor, scor was a renegade... his men were ruthless and cut throat he took no prisoners and when he did? He only extracted info and for selfish gain and then executed them and had no shame...

One day...

"coby! Come in for dinner! The night is setting in!"

Coby came galloping coby was a bundle of joy at a young age...

"coming mom!"

"hey kiddo, have some dinner"

He coby came from the backyard and the sun was setting and one of the three moons were peaking their heads above the horizon... dad was watching the news about the crisis on scor and scor was raising an army and was preparing to invade... coby's father, harry, was a little anxious...

Coby came into the living room distracted by dad's "habit..." mother, abbey, came into the room...

"cant you watch something else?" coby and harry eye struck as abbey complained...

"honey?"

Henry's 8th book

— 52 —

"HARRY!!!"
"Yes, dear?"
"Harry? Your son is watching this, have you no restraint?"
"BABE?" (pulling out his unlit cigar from his mouth...)(liked the smell)
"babe? Listen, if were to stop this tribe of vicious people, from the start, we have to know about it and 2 if we don't know about it, I mean how can you solve the problem if you don't know about it???"
"fine, harry? For our son then..."
"which will have no future if these people get what they want!"
(getting up from his smoking chair complaining as he gently paced)

Later that month coby was in home-school after a savage attack on the school by scor fanatics

Henry's 8th book

— 53 —

When coby was 16 he was playing ball with the team...
"pitch it!" swoosh! Clap! "Strike! You're out!"
The crowd cheered and as the coach came out in despair, he came up to coby who lost the game and struck out...
"coby? You know what your parents say: 'winning isn't everything...'
Its not all true... coby? I'm gonna have to let you go..."
Ah hell chief? I can do this! Just give me a chance!"
"ive been giving you so many chances for 8 months, maybe your not cut out for this you don't quite fir the profile I'm sorry kid, you're out...

However he was dissapointed but he was strong in heart and didn't give up he may have had to leave ball but that would not drag him down and even after the strike and the game lost and the great disappointment on the day...

When he was 18 he joined the military... all the while the rebels were trying to break the barriers of the border wall set up to slow the assault of scor during the whole period of time coby was surrounded by the culture of defending his country from the evil scor throughout his life he was surrounded and this day of recruitment was the time of the service to his country...

Thats when he earned a military degree in weapons research and he studied under his commander and he was like a father to him... he learned how to make and dismantle bombs and how to disarm them he then became fluent in bombing arts he then made masters in nuclear bombs and became fluent in hydrogen weapons specialist

Later that year while hearing of the news of scor he was prompted of a secret meeting of the enemy about high profile nuclear bombs and hydrogen weaponry, 40 of them, all over the bordering neighboring countries
He was listening in on the meeting by radio frequency
"we have um..."
"When do we order the strike?"
"soon..."
"What does master scor say?"

"He said lay the control room with booby traps so no one can stop the process in case of a breach..."

" now after all we've suffered we will finally have justice"

Coby stuttered: "oh no! Oh GOD!" Said coby in a panic!
He told the commander and the commander thought and then spoke to his officials then they decided to send coby in...

"we'll be sending you in to stop this attack, hell or high water!"

Later in the 4th day of the week...

Coby was sent in to infiltrate the base to the control code room to dismantle the missile strike operations

Henry's 8th book

*BAM!! BAM!! CHE CHE CHE!!
CLICK 123, WHEW! TINK TINK! BLAM!!!
Fall IN! FALL IN! GO GO GO!!!
CHUG CHUG CHUG!!! BLAM!!!*

The enemy shot back while yelling "you'll never take us alive!!!! you little bastards!!!"
"GO GO!!!" the troopers filed in to get the very protected coby into the control room...

They came up to the control room slapped c4 on the door latch "doot doot" BLAST!!!

"Alright I'm in!!!"
Surprisingly the door suddenly latched shut behind him! The troopers could not reopen the latched door!

Henry's 8th book

— 58 —

Meanwhile coby being helpless got straight to work dismantling the launch codes and closed down the launching sequence...

Suddenly and sadly... the room filled with toxic poisonous gas and as he tried to hold his breath? He slowly choked to death after successfully decoding the bombs....

When the commander heard of this heroism? "my peer, my son? saved us all..."

"to this day to this day" the commander spoke: "today we honor the sacrifice of all men and women who gave of themselves to serve our country... today we celebrate coby... a most unfamiliar figure...however this statue stands for someone who rescued the world without coby our

planet would be scarred for ever more we honor this wonderful person... whom I loved like a son..." he started to cry... the commander left the podium weeping for his country and for the loss and sacrifice of coby... and there they honored coby for his gift to all mankind...

THE END...

OH! MORNING LIGHT!

dedicated to my savior whom loves me with an everlasting love.... in the dawning light as the sun will rise, it shines so bright as the twilight dies... so! I raise my voice! to the sky, so bright! in the morn's light! for I will seek his face and answer him... and he! will too! answer brave... and so, we shall meet at the shores so great! that we shall see the twinkling' at first morn's eternal fate! for the morning star casts its shining face! down onto the ocean waves! as we walk along an I see his face? and as we speak in no haste, as we glide in grace? so, that there we are in his light? OH??!! his morn's light? as I and he? walk the shores of grace? I shall forever seek his face....... MAY GOD, THE LORD JESUS, BE BLESSED FOREVER AND MY LOVE IS FOR HIM.... I LOVE YOU JESUS! I WILL ALWAYS LOVE YOU

To you my Annie...

To you my Annie to you...with eyes so blue hair so fair skin so soft and heart so gentle... is there anyone so sweet as you? One who rules the galaxies with such grace...teardrops fall as you are guided into my arms, a fair maiden, warrior and queen!oh fair maiden ruler of the universe and a doe of the desert... is there anyone so fair as you??? hair falls like dry grasses of the yellow meadow, grasses of the windy fields your grace like the oceans tide...your mind filled with heavens starlit jewelry, gems pearls and diamonds, glistening in the deep of space...your heart wild and free as a prancing doe that prances to its destiny... it eats of the wild oats and drinks the rivers water...and when you cry... your tear drops fall like heavens rain... falling onto a dry and desperate   thirst desert hoping and happy for the rain... you are truly grace and love... for all that is...that is all that matters... to me? My gracious love... Annie to you my love...to you... -Henry...

RAIN...

The day was young... the hour was bright and the rain was sweet... As the rain fell... the flowers opened to beautiful yellow bursting sunlight... The trees were wet with dew so too the grass and the flowers were gently soaked with the noon day rain... and a slight flowing breeze coursed through the cool moist air... AND! As the deer lept through the furry ferns and bushes... their hair was matted with gentle rain falling onto their grace filled backs and as the sun set to the end of the day? The sun shone rays of brilliant golden orange streaks through the falling drops of the rain... And so the night had begun...

Suffering

Dear lord GOD! I suffer most every day... all day long I groan trapped in a desert place... a desert of the spirit...all things I have suffered have been for loss all the year left alone to die... no remorse no empathy no happiness   or fulfillment every day I weep wanting to go back home to heaven... my spirit languishes in this desert... and I have no home... I desperately cry out to you OH! GOD! Where are you? Why have you left me here? I have no goal, no destination, no feeling of hope?

Where are you oh my lord? For you! You! Oh wonderful Majesty have control and power and omnipotence over all things in the universe... thus I sit here in regret and brokenness...yet I will look to the heavens for there yet is still hope and hope for me...for my love is in heaven...waiting for me to come to him... may his beauty and Majesty forever be exalted   forever and ever exalted for he alone is GOD ALMIGHTY!!

Blessed be the name of the LORD of LORDS and king of kings

AMEN AND AMEN

Henry's 8th book

— 65 —

Shores of twilight

The sun was a brilliant blaze on the seas horizon the wind was light   and cool and the suns light was split only by the orange morning mist of the twilight... the oceans tide was a gentle and relaxing melody... and as the sea waded and waxed on the shore, walked those eternal shores of gentle peace... as the two walked the shore with bare feet safely on the moist sand that nestled into their toes... with love in the midst, they enjoyed the love shared by the two of them... the cool morning air blowing in their hair coursing waves, a gentle breeze that left their heads a comfortable cool heads Thus they walked by the shore to their hearts content and off they went...

ODD OR EVEN

Players: 1-10
Pieces: 3 dice, chips or money
Game type: Gambling game
Direction: counter clock wise

First, all players choose who goes first... then, the first player rolls 3 dice to start... if the whole amount of the dice is even? The player receives the whole amount in coins or chips and if the amount is odd the player receives nothing... the player rolls only 3 times... the player if money to have to bet? Chooses to bet or not...if he has no money to bet hes for-fit his play...

When he rolls, player can choose to bet any amount up to all he has or down to as little he has...

He then while rolling or shaking dice in hand calls out to the table of players: "ODD!" or "EVEN!"

After calling out he drops the dice... if he is right? He doubles the bet and receives double the bet... and takes his allotment... if hes wrong? He loses all the money and the bank holds to the next wager and the next player if he wins he receives what ever the player before him lost and his own winnings if the next player loses the bank holds his earnings for the next player and the turns circulate in this fashion...

Players circulate till all players are eliminated down to one last player or

until each player decides to stop or get for-fit his play
Players can choose to continue to watch the play till play has ended...

If play has continued for some time? Players can agree to end their session.. and thus end their play in the game...

<u>*DAVID*</u>

One day David was playing football he dived for the ball caught it! "you cant catch this one!!!"
When he launched the ball it went all the way to the goal... "your good damn good.."
Mike said

Henry's 8th book

Mean while...
KORR was an alien and his complexion was fierce and frightening and his eye a fiery piercing purple...
He was speaking to a large crowd on his home planet...
"my people! I shall see as you shall see that as time passes in my rule it will become more apparent that there are life forms on other planets that either need to be conquered or annihilated by other neighboring systems we will conquer we will destroy and with the might of our power we shall conquer the galaxy!!!if you do not agree or if you reject this order to haunt and destroy neighboring planets?your life be for-fit and you will be burned alive..."

He was always trying to manipulate the people and tear them down the people of the planet felt so much political pressure that they grieved together in secret to avoid the burning stocks a fiery death... So they were forced into military service and submission...

Jessica, a woman who had doubts of GODS sacred love... a woman who had lost hope in her heart...while losing direction in having multiple relations creating a void of purpose in her life... It left her severely abused and depressed... she, after walking away from her purpose for many years came back and wanted to know that life could be better on this side and the next life to come...

One day David was crying and Jessica was watching behind the ferny bush... and as the angel came up to David and comforted David

"how lord? Why? Why does the lord want to ruin something so precious as to the planet???"
He deeply wept
"OH LORD!!! WHY!"
The angel replied: "David? Your name means beloved... and that you are... oh David... you're deeply loved by him that hovered above the darkness of the deepness of the waters below and raised the airy seas of the heavens do not be alarmed... you are safe... you have been heard...and the lord will answer yes to your prayer... he will restore the planet and not destroy it..."

As the angel of the LORD spoke concerning David and his future hope the angel of GOD made clear to David that the planet shall not die in his generation yet be preserved while he dwelt in it...

Thus the angel left in a bright immense but, immediate striking flash and with a burst of brilliant bright white light, yet only to freckle in a sparkle away...

Jessica did not come out, yet hid... she saw a glimmer of hope in the midst of David...
She hated what she had become...she had hated what she had become...

She needed help that was for sure...

Meanwhile David was having trouble with the pastor of his home church whom kicked him out of church for he was too idealistic and didn't listen... so he was alone in solitude...
But then...

— 73 —

"recent reports say that an alien craft half the size of the moon is heading straight toward us!!!"

Another report said:"news coming in yes, reports are coming in that the large flat arrow head shaped ships slowing down I repeat they are slowing down!!!"

David went outside to see the ships...

As the ships settled into an orbit something happened right before the invasion...

A blue speck like a star appeared before the entire planet it hovered into orbit but the star seemed to search for something it moved back and forth as if it was searching for something suddenly it hovered to a stop over Davids city...

The star started to descend... as it descended, it found a place to land... it was night... the blue star spoke and every time he spoke the star would give off a blue shine an emanating glory to the place it surrounded

When the star was fully descended he called out to David...
"DAVID... I AM THAT I AM..."

"I AM THAT I AM HAS SENT FOR YOU TO DEFEND ALL LIFE ON THIS PLANET..."
"DAVID!!!!! COME INTO MY LIGHT!!!"

Henry's 8th book

— 75 —

So David without question- went in...

As David was secure in the star went slowly hovering upward in the heavens As the star was approaching the ships, the ships attacked the star with no relent and fired multiple rounds at the star yet the star was untouched by any of the ships... the star was mystically   was impervious   to any attack blasting from the ships weaponry...

So David and the star joined in some strange bond and David stretched out his arm toward the ships and thus the ship like by command crackled apart like scattering debris, then! The last ship trying to pull out all the stops- however to no avail no attack would prevail... and thus David destroyed with korr on the ship breath his last and the enemy was defeated with a flick of the wrist...

*As the star hovered down? He, the star released David to gentle ground
David had just saved the entire planet*

He was in a hospital bed recovering, as he recovered, Jessica snuck in while David was sleeping   and looked even stared! Jessica had her prayers answered by this David whom by the golden lit hill met an angel whom answered Davids and jessicas prayers

"THE PLANET SHALL NOT DIE TODAY!!!" the angel spoke over David in memory...

David was a man that believed what he held right and true... so faithful a man he

Henry's 8th book

put himself on the line to do what was right and to what he believed in that's only half the story... I AM had to favor him as well the angel of the LORD

After the testing of Davids faith he lived out his days in peace and his promise given to him by the LORD and the LORD kept him forever more...

THE END

DESIRE...

To you my love I call out...of you? When will I see? To embrace thee ...my love my diamond eye... for to be with you, is all my dreams, all I could ever ask for... you are wonderful, lovely my dear... do not fret

my loving lady my roe... my tenderness in my very own heart...
Before the universe, was ever founded, YOU! Were in my inmost deepest DESIRE...
Plans to prosper you and lift you up... my love? Where have you gone my love? I feel low
I feel?... worthless... worthless without you!!! I NEED your loving kindness for I am bankrupt without your love...

I love you dear thank you for all that you do and all that you've done...

THE BEAUTY OF CREATION

The flowers and the tulips... The garden and the ferns... The green and the gold... The grasses of the field... The trees and the bright furry bushes... The animals of the forest... The blue skies and the golden sunsets And the little cubs of nature... The hope in the air... All these objects of creation... All these beauties, the hope of creation... And the hope of breath given to us... For ours is to have and to hold... For our enjoyment and pleasure- to live life in the full, the purpose of creation, the plan of existence The hope of salvation Blessings...

THE BEGININNG ...

The time had come... the new season had just begun And a new chapter of life had opened... It was time And out of death new born life!! A newborn cry, as sorrow had razed The truth had dawned It was a new beginning, thus it was so!!! And the golden path to ever after had started! And out of the ashes came refreshing HOPE...

Henry's 8th book

— 81 —
<u>The Dreams We Dream...</u>

As we lie down, our eyes rest... the visions of the twilight Inspiring scenes of the glory of the night... The WHEELS propel The camera obscures and the fortune tells... Tis' the dreams we dream... An epiphany of Excellency and majesty As the early morning dawn arises The dark night fades And a new glory to the dreams we dream THE Morning...

Henry's 8th book

— 82 —
THE LORDS LOVE...

To me? You are beautiful…. there is nothing, no one, or anything that could shake us We are one… we shall never end… stand on me… depend on me… I am here.. for you… Dear heart? Dear? Listen… I miss you so… I love you… hold my hand? Dear? Never give up on me??? because I love you my dear… I am here for you? Never lose hope? For I am your strong hand… I am here… I will never forsake you? For I am the LORD… whom will never forget you…see? I have inscribed you on the palms of my hand? Dear soul? I shall hold you thru all of the pain…. thru all the chaos, for I am a strong tower and shelter… never let go for I and my strong arm have you…. never let go or lose hope? Because I have you and you are safe…

— 83 —

Never leave for even in your stress I have you through it all... Sing to me, cry to me hold to me... for I am strong and merciful... and I know the road... do not worry... I am a very present help in times of trouble...

And it was the day...

it was the morning the beginning there in the twilight... the flowers were blooming...the deer were foraging on the tulips the dew rinsing the plants and luscious flowers in their mouths moist and sweet, an aroma emanating from their wet mouths a perfume as they ate of the fruit of the fields...the sun just beginning there streak across the twilight covered sky... a bright morning gaze across the morning horizon the morning commute had just began and so the town was all abuzz across this small city as light cast beams of yellow streaks touching the tip of the small town and on the wet soil in the farm land and local greenery... the roosters crow could be heard... as the earths song the crowing of a rooster began it was a sign to all a sign of old...

The sign that the day had just begun...

And it was the day
JEREMY...

The New Beginning...

Twas' the time of love... Twas' the time of hope... And the hope of nations... There the children of nations, tribes, and people! Sing! Sing to GOD in Heaven! For the year of the LORD has come! And now! There is much rejoicing praise and worship! FOR! The GOD of GODS has triumphed over evil and darkness and the light of hope has come to set the men of the earth free!!! Tis' the year of the LORD... and the hope of nations the future of our GOD and the peace of nations! Tis' the time of hope! The time of love... The hope of nations has begun... The beginning...

THE ONE TRUE CONSTANT:

Through out all time there has always been a common constant that does not vary, like a hope that does not waver in the winds of change... This constant knows no bounds The elegance of this constants flow? Is the objective of love... Love is at the point of common hope a -standard- that cant be generally computed Yet is at the very heart of common: HOPE, FAITH, PEACE, JOY, AND HOLLOWED SPIRIT OF GOODNESS...(a GOD-like spirited strength...) The love of GOD is the center of the binding of our hope, the ultimate GOD like RATIO The basis of truth... The hope of beautiful hearts The payment of faith bound in sacrifice... LOVE IS THE ANSWER...

the stars...

broken am I broken, broken I cry! and who can put me back together again???!!!! years and years! only to die a broken death! as I pass through this season knowing my fate... I await my death till everyone leaves me and I pass and there lo'! and behold JESUS! there HE is waiting for me on the shores of eternal grace!!! there is nothing but nothing to nothing... all is dust and love is eternal... all I remember is those stars.... those stars shine for me... every night.... I look up to the stars.... hoping to see that beauty my

Henry's 8th book

— 88 —

beauty my love.... my true love.. the one who cares for me really...Kristy... my special secret admirer my beloved.... the only one who knows.... the only one.... he says they shine for me.... he tells me he loves me and I had no clue.... he knows... he wants me... I miss him...I want to go HIS heaven... I will look up at the sky at night watching the stars as the day goes and the stars pop out as I am homeless begging on the street no hope... I will look to the heavens and see the beauty of the majesty of GOD and liken it to HIS love for me so... when I pass? I will walk that bridge to heaven crying in passion of sadness and longing... only to cry out in happiness and joy... and I will walk that bridge to heaven to my home and into heaven I will walk.... into the gates of home I will slumber... as I rest in his gates in the stars of GOD... the stars of GOD the blessed stars of the LORD GOD... and there I will reside... and forever rest with my savior... my love.... blessings...

<u>To my dear savior.</u>
dear savior... dear, dear savior... how I love thee... you are my special guy... you surround me with your arms and you comfort me with you loving kindness.... there is no one like you that could otherwise bring me peace of mind.... in the midst of the forces in my pain in my solitary confinement, you bring me solace... is there anyone like you? your heart makes you glow.... you shine like the stars of heaven.... in my hurt you are

there to comfort me... when I'm down you are there to wipe away my tears.... you wait for me... you're shy like me... we talk we laugh in my heart we do, we know!... we know.... that in my heart you will always reside..... you're there glowing.... patient, faithful.... loving, cute, kind never to disturb, always there to help in the best of ways.... is there anyone so greatly kind in your beauty? as you? no.... you're beautiful... in all ways in my sadness you sit by me safely guard me you see every tear..... you see every sin every wicked thing and you know what I've done wrong.... and I know! but for a while... but you know for good BUT! does that change how you think of me? NO.... you love me just the same you show your loving affection in all the ways you do.... just to know I'm special even when I'm not perfect and you tell me the stars shine for me even when I don't... I'm surprised by

— 91 —

your soft kind love and affection that you share with me you save me even when I don't realize it... you rescue everyone everywhere a little bit a day and slowly but surely you'll win our hearts as you have been here for us in our hearts guiding us to make the right decisions tell us where to go and lead us beside still waters... you're the real hero.... who's the real hero? who is it! who is my love???? you.... you have been the one all along slowly guiding me to you to your spoken heart filled word of mouth? HOW kind? to lead me back to the bible verses that speak of your love? what that will last forever is your kind love that can't be replaced by anyone or anything..... it is said.... that everything and everyone has its place in the universe? for you? you hold a very special place in our hearts minds and souls you will never give up on us nor leave us or ever forsake us? how special you are? to me and all fellow men truly you are the reason for life itself that over shadows all things.... because of your amazing love... I LOVE YOU MY DEAR SAVIOR..... MY SAVIOR OF MY HEART.... - Henry beloved...

TO THE BROKEN HEART

Love, true love, my dear, WILL NEVER FAIL you, Dear love? for tho a shell of a lie may crack apart and disappoint you? listen to my lovely Word? when everything falls apart and your life is in turmoil and your friends desert you? everyone forsakes you? and your left all alone?... love my dear? WILL NEVER FAIL YOU OR Let you down... Never give up...

To the solemn night...

To the solemn night... as the sea waxes and wades in the twilight and the moon drifts across the sky your stars lit next to the darkness and the clouds parting and joining... and as the crickets of the twilight begin their loud resonation before the earthy forest, the owls begin their whooping watch of the darkness... yes to thew night for the night is darkest before the dawning light and as the illuminating morning begins the night ends the dawn begins its ascent consuming the darkness of the night... to

the night, yes to the night... for all times have their purpose and meaning beginning   and ending... thus after the darkness comes the light and after the night the dawn
The morning...

<u>WE ARE!!!</u>

Oh how the days have gone by... the people suffer for lack of bread the ocean wades... the sun is covered...the hour grows dark... is there any hope? When this mortal life shall cease? And I decay? and what to others? Will I not care? How can anyone do right? "tis' hard (but glorious) to be poor and honest... an empty sack can hardly stand upright; but if the sack stands?" dear wonder! How?

Henry's 8th book

*Why? And what for? And for who?
Whether we are strong or weak??? Fair or
modest? What difference does it make?
WE ALL SUFFER...but the in the eastern
New York harbor there is hope...and with
life (as long as we have it), we are
strong... we ARE AMERICANS... and we
are powerful only when we stand
together we are the family of GOD, hard
pressed, bloody, sanctified, tested, tried
and true...
American freedom... WERE TOUGH! And
we
never give in!!! were the home of the free
land of the brave
and dwelling of the strong and we are the
hope of nations...
GOD BLESS THE UNITED STATES OF
AMERICA -Henry*

Henry's 8th book

THE DAWN...

The morning was fragrant with the sweet smell of roses and tulips, the sun, rising in the east breaking through the clouds splashing beams of light through the trees and bushes , sprinkling light from the water droplets everywhere... the doe and buck were nestled in the ferns and high grass, munching on weeds in the ferny forest... the chipmunks resonating a morning chatter the blessed the environment
And the wind was only a twiddle to the dandelions   the trees soaked up the dew left by a midnight rain... it was the morning it was to far to tell- and the day had just begun...

Henry's 8th book

— 97 —

It was the dawn...

WHOM SHALL I SEND

Dear roost?dear dear roost? Oh how I want you? How I cling to you how I want you...there is no one greater... no one like you? HOW HOW!!! HOW SEAS HAVE RAVAGED MY WILDERNESS!! I have hated everything... how I have lost so much...how I have fallen...with nothing, nothing left! Dear heaven my dear heavens? My home roost! My only home for my heart! Oh how I have been lost in the ravages!!! What soul is this?! who's livelihood are rags in the desolate... how

Henry's 8th book

— 98 —

my soul dries up in the waters of nothingness rags of emptiness battle after languishing rotten battle!!! to my desperate last stand!!! in this aching loneliness of a desert!!! to do all I can to save that which he cant!!! Oh my soul! Never dying jealousy And envy of emptiness!!! WHY??!! WHY??!! WHY Father? WHY I CANT GIVE UP NOW!! AND NOW THAT THE BATTLE IS OVER? Oh Lord oh LORD what end? To what end?!! I languish after all that is green and good in the world... OH HOW I HAVE FORSAKEN MYSELF FOR THE SAKE OTHERS!!!! Now all that is gold is death And my aches in the land of the forgotten My sword fallen! My shield broken... MY PLEA AS I FLY!!! "SAVE ME PLEASE!!!" IM FALLING!!! I wait as my eyes darken... THE LORD OF LORDS CRIES OUT A DESPARATE PLEA!!! " WHOM SHALL I SEND!!!!" FIN

Henry's 8th book

— 99 —

YOU...

Oh lord your love is unfailing you show me power in your love yet so beautiful, oh how you shine...
Humanity cheers, for you embrace sin for humanity... for your love knows no bounds... no one hinders you and nothing hinders you... your power in love is limitless... you bend space and time by prevailing winds and supernatural forces!!! your beauty is seen in the control

Henry's 8th book

— 100 —

of the supernatural! Your glistening red brown hair is as young as a morning dove... a young morning dove... your manliness shines as glistening beauty in your power... your wonderful in all your ways... you are lovely in strength and beauty is in your deep blue eyes of an oceans mist... I love your love   you are a a lovely aroma a fair scent... a fragrance in the midst of the air...
Thank you lord for all that you do...
Thank you LORD

Henry's 8th book

— 101 —
And the day began...

As the doe hopped through the alfalfa her baby dear lept behind... and as the sun rose, the fields sparkled with dew it was a chilly morning the night rained to the day to welcome morning creatures to a sweet moist luscious leafy breakfast with berry's abounding the moon was a dimming waning   gibbous copper coin in the fading twilight... the birds enjoying the elemental surroundings   there the birds praised the nature with their voices and chirps of cuteness only to add to the greatness of the beauty of nature that quickly   was immersed in all the beautiful surroundings... as if nature had been   joyfully surprised and yet only to welcome the idea of its own beauty

Henry's 8th book

— 102 —

And the day began...
-Jeremy

Twilight rhyme

As the sun would rise the night has died and the twilight hides

Henry's 8th book

— 103 —

Thus the morning greets the sun so sweet on the mountaintops those gentle mountaintops
So I gaze a glare so brave on the trees so great that the twinkling of the stars so dim   I see the mornings rim... a rainbow in the west as it bears its best... an army of colors a tapestry of glory that the morning cannot compare with such a glorious glare the clouds part the bright sky the morning begins ans the twilight sings

And the day begins as the morning ends

Thus from every beginning, there is some beginnings end...
-Henry

DAWN

The moon was a bright orange disc in the sky... all the crickets were singing in the night scenery
There the stars were twinkling a chatter on a black backdrop. Lighting the sky like twinkling firefly's
As the earth spun the night stars flew over the canvas sky as the night time passed...
The moon slowly spun thru from horizon to horizon over the dark period...some parting clouds a deep and quiet ocean blue lit by the moon passed across the sky morphing as they went
A wind blew a cool chill on the surface of the earth...
The owls were excited for it... thew very beginning of the dawn had begun

*Softly gently the moon's light had
dimmed quietly and slowly dissipated
along with the stars
Only to have the morning light replace
and follow the night
A morning rainbow of rising color had
engulfed the twilight the sun had risen
thus the moon was a faint crescent in the
sky, the sun had risen and it was the
dawn*

NIGHT SKY

*As the sun set the slight wind blew
coursing waves through the long dry
grasses... and there... he lay in the evening
air enjoying the twilight sky... the windy
air blew softly through his wavy red*

Henry's 8th book

brown hair... dreaming in the starlight he was next to his black pickup watching the sky turn from periwinkle to a deep blue to a deep blue to a dark blue the dark gathered around him only to have the brightly lit stars twinkle in whites and blues and oranges and reds and there over a period of some time in the middle of this dry grassy land! Bloom's the milky way galaxy! A cosmic phenomena engulfing with brilliance and beauty! the luminous intoxication of the night sky softer than a crickets call... it shone over the dark night sky like a beautiful blanket covering the sky with soft light... as he jack, lay in the sweet perfume of the night? He drifted off to sleep...

Who knew where his dreams would take him till morn's end...

Sunset journey

It was nice   in the cool evening in late October
The green leaves only to lose their ripe glory the sun had set and everything was ablaze in the late evening sky the clouds a fiery red... a broken sky... as he stood before the glory of the blazing sunset an explosion across the western horizon... he was only darkened   a silhouette against the fiery backdrop of this totally GOD endowed glory...he breathed in deep and sighed as the cool wind brushed his red brown hair as he proppt up against

Henry's 8th book

— 108 —

the rock then he left that rock and walked into the sunset on his journey he would have never known what he may run into... as he blazed the remarkable trail his mind could only have imagined where this path would take him...
Jeremy

<u>**DUSK**</u>

There... the wind was slowly breathing through the grassy fields like waves of wind coursing through in waves of the watery depths... the sun was just under the mountains horizon... gleaming beams of yellow gray light through the mountains scapes, shining through the clouds as streaks across the twilight sky... the pines were waving in the wind... the melody resonating through the air of the tree tops... the clouds over the time darkened to a fluffy 'blue-white' as the sun lost its grip on the power of the twilight over the brightness of the clouds...   the daffodil's slowly closed by the mountainous chill of   darkening sky and slowly and surely the star began their ascent   and luminous twinkle over the canvas up above and the night had just begun

And it was the night...

Henry's 8th book

— 110 —

Morns glory

The mornings glow was a show put on display as the suns rays show the way the shining light was so bright that the bursting rays blasted the day! The mornin glow shined to and fro to light up the up the way for lo the suns glow was for the doe to show which way for a meal sowed for the deer young and old as if found so treasured as of gold so the nature ate like kings as the eternal bells ringed for the day was only the beginning for the

Henry's 8th book

morning had just begun over the sky so early on for some morning's eternal story

The storm

The rain tapped the tin roof under the dark cloudy sky the darkened view was very gloomy... the ponderosa trees heavily waving in the strong winds and the rain fell almost sideways...
It was cold...the rain and wind together soaked the area... the wind only chilled the conditions... lightning popped thru the fierce sky!!! pop! Crack! Crackle!! Booom... inside the newly wed couple were trying to stay warm by the chimney run fire... the snaps and crackles of the

fire were only quiet reminders of the storms around them... suddenly a chill ran up them in their blankets. Lightening Blasted across the sky!! crack!!! BOOOM! As they shivered in their beds! The fire warmed them after their insulated area collected heat the shed was suddenly much warmer then they slept thru the storm....

A star Is born

In the dark there, there in the midst sparkling darkness the lights in the darkening midst lay a field of stars in a

Henry's 8th book

sparkling abyss , covered in shining glowing clouds light being shed in every dark corner... light spread over the milky glowing clouds , and there! Suddenly! A massive silent explosion shook the milky abyss all in a round quiet blast echoing outwards in all directions! And there out of the dust! In a great passage of time!! A STAR IS BORN!!!!the sparkling surroundings sparkled glittered in little speckles! And! As the residue rested all around the new star...thus the dust accumulated around the new star thus a new begging of life and life it would be! A star is born...

Henry's 8th book

— 114 —

<u>The little boy</u>

As the earth orbits the sun the planets in all there glowing glory the sun and all its glory- the sun and all its glory... shining so brightly! Casting glory to glory as it shines from mercury to Venus to earth in all their splendor from earth to mars   yet a shining specktical still! Jupiter to Saturn Saturn to Uranus to Neptune Neptune to Pluto a faint dimming star the sun proclaim little glory and past that the Oort cloud a faint prick of light and beyond? To a scene of nebula and clouds and pockets of milky light covered in sparkles of light? And beyond? To a scene? So marvelous and so spectacular! So unimaginable!   The glory of all glories JESUS! At the center of it all! The corner stone has become the very capstone!!!

placed like a bright luminous mantle!! ON THAT OLD TESTED TRIED AND TRUE ROCK!!!! "forgive them father for they do not know what they do! The middle of that shining galaxy! Yet to the center of every galaxy! An example of pure humility... and true love... and an example the center of every piece of the universe- the beginning from earth to the ends and center of the existence that is known to THE FATHER- a glimmer...

A glimmer in the new born eye a glimmer in the heart of all creation to the beginning of the universe!
And there...
In the image of GOD a twinkle of light...
A twinkle of light in a little boy- writing to hid daddy...
"i love you daddy? Do you hear me?...
Eternity...

Arthur

One day he was walking home from school... as always he was hiding from bullies...he was coming up to his house... and he saw his dad! "hey kiddo! I need a helping hand with this firewood got time?" "daddy!" he chuckled... his son Arthur jumped all over him... they stacked the wood at the end of the afternoon when it was dark Arthur watched the snow fallout from the inside... as he sipped hot cocoa his mother made him "Arthur" mother voiced " come for dinner!"
The contents of the cup wobbled as he set it down in the window sill (gallop gallop tromp tromp)
As he went frolicking and galloping towards his mother...

*OK OK hold your pants on! Tessa teased...
mommy mommy! Whats for dinner? The
father came in to see all the commotion
"whats all this ruckus?"
"Oh! My boy you little rascal?"
They enjoyed a home cooked spaghetti
dinner and some home made strudel pie...
As the night twiddled away, dawn arose
while they slept a peaceful night...*

*At their bedside   was a cat named Sam
and a dog named spot both cuddled up to
the beds near the fire
Spot on his Matt and SAM on his nest the
fire crackled near their bodies...
The sun crept near the horizon and the
midnight snow had crystallized   and the
sun warmed the ground
To the point of dew....then outside in the
upper atmosphere the clouds poured dew
onto the earth as the rain accumulated in
the clouds...the wind blew and the rain*

fell… thunder, quiet, but deep and distant could be heard as it echoed thru the sky… it was a rainy Saturday morning in the pine forest and they were getting ready for going to the store as Arthur   his shoes on dad,helped   Dan was was getting Arthur ready for shopping for a new pair of shoes and a little snack for a little Arthur…

As they were driving thru the melting snowy asphalt
Paved roads cold and windy inside the vehicle   however was a much different story as Arthur watched as the rain pummeled the side window in his safety seat… " mom dad are we there yet?"
"we'll be there soon sweetie"
He begun to kick his feet twiddling to himself
When he got to the store they shopped for the necessities and a lollipop for

Henry's 8th book

Arthur the next day was a Sunday and that's when everything changed...

As Daniel was late for work driving in a very frustrating blizzard... suddenly out of the white blizzard mist!!!
BLAM!

White light surrounded Daniel "im floating"
As Daniel felt peace all around with a bright white light   in the distance...
"DANIEL..."
Who are you?
'I AM THAT I AM..."
"I HAVE SENT FOR YOU"
"COME UP HERE"
Dan was taken up... on that very hour...
"mom?"
"yes officer, thank you..."

Henry's 8th book

— 120 —

Tessa was in sheer shock heartache UN bearable and in dis-
belief but soon the realization surely sunk in...
"honey?" Tessa voiced in heartache and held Arthur by his chin gently, saying...
There something I have to tell you...

Many weeks spread finally thru the most coaching as much with a child that you can
Arthur had gripped the fatal realization in deep agony...

"MOMMY MOMMY!

Where did he go mommy?"
Tears streamed down his face...
The resolve was final as well as the realization of the loss...

Henry's 8th book

Arthur was dead inside for some time...
Soon school would resume   as usual
and dear coping would continue
He persevered and he was a strong child...

Years later Arthur was outside with spot
WHISTLE! "here spot!"
He made for a steady strong backed
teenager...

"come on spot!" spot came in as a very
jolly dog...
years later to the present dads passing
had been rough his memory of his dad
was a sweet melody and aroma in his
mind...
Tho it was rough his family was steady
and strong...

"WHY MOM?! WHY NOW?!"

"im Alone and your father would have wanted this..."

"Son hes gone... hes gone Arthur and your old enough to accept this..."

"mom! No!"-son its time to move on, do this for your dad do it for me...

Arthur was stewing over mothers decision

Spot came up to Arthur licking him continuously
Over time spot considered Arthur to be the man of the house...

As well as Arthur...
  He wasn't ready to open up
It had been years and what he had been used to was dissolving

Henry's 8th book

His heart was breaking- "but that's love, " I haven't lost you yet daddy?"

"SON... LET GO..." he heard it in his very heart... "there! There it is again?" "SON... LET ME GO...." "DAD?" "SON"

A week passed the red Subaru slowly pulled into the forested driveway... Tessa stressed and a little overwhelmed closing the side door with groceries in hand... Arthur was 15 (not quite enough to drive)
"hey mom whatdgya get?"
"oh... enough..." they hurdled thru the door- 5 inches deep of snow...
"Here yah go boy, " "thanks mom..."
AS they tracked the snow into the front door ,spot came rushing in   and the fire crackled... after Tessa stressed of Arthur "plain and tall" TO get his"BUTT"   to putting away the groceries... then Tessa

rested on dads old chair as she sat the phone rang...it was- him... "OH! HI... no im not...tonight?
Hmm hmm... sure ill see you then... hmm thank you   your so sweet... oh OK bye..."

Later in the evening: "yes mom you look great...don't worry hell like the dress go go go... she cried out and hugged Arthur: "oh Arthur! Thank you!!

As time passed they had grown fond of Grieg and over time Greg had grown on Arthur...

Tho Greg could never replace Dan they grew to be friends even to brothers

Every year mom Greg and Arthur accepted the future hope of their family rebuilt and every year they paid tribute to their taken father

They would pay tribute to Dan the beloved favor and memory of their first begotten love of Dan

There at the grave of Dan the sun was setting causing rays of beautiful yellow streaking across the horizon a tribute for Dan every time the sun shined on his beloved resting bed...

The end...

Henry's 8th book

Oh my friend!

Oh my friend I love you my heart is in deep pain... I need you!my heart sings heartbreak... everything I do my love for you? Tears my heart to bloody shreds... blood pours from my shredded chest...yet? My heart pours bloody love... have I lost you? Have I lost you... my spirit bleeds and my flesh is dead... my heart- shredded. Im wrecked!
I die in this deadly desert plain... every day in this desert searching for my rose? My red desert rose without the thorns there is

Henry's 8th book

— 127 —

no blossom with out pain there is no love oh my blessed rose? I bleed for you... im falling... will! will you catch me...
-Henry

In the deep...

There in the deep abyss, there... a twinkle of light in the morning a bright star... shining in the lavender twilight! And slowly the star shone over the glistening horizon lessening over the the brightening silhouette... then! As the dim star faded! The bright morning star! Shined while the morning bell rang out to welcome the suns rising to greet the glow with music music to the heavens... sorrow had been thru the night in an instant of an a twinkling of an eye joy comes in the morning as the sun rises the world at an end... grace is as heaven bound as the heavens rejoice! Jesus comes to take his elect away to break the chains and set free the captive glory glory to GOD the father for his marvelous work joy to the heaven bound!!! peace...peace to all... Blessings...

www.ingramcontent.com/pod-product-compliance
Lightning Source LLC
Chambersburg PA
CBHW020434220526
45464CB00002B/697